My FUTURE CAREER

Working with
Children

Margaret McAlpine

GARETH**STEVENS**
GS
P U B L I S H I N G
A World Almanac Education Group Company

Please visit our web site at: **www.garethstevens.com**
For a free color catalog describing Gareth Stevens Publishing's
list of high-quality books and multimedia programs, call
1-800-542-2595 (USA) or 1-800-387-3178 (Canada).
Gareth Stevens Publishing's fax: (414) 332-3567.

Library of Congress Cataloging-in-Publication Data

McAlpine, Margaret.
        Working with children / Margaret McAlpine.
            p. cm. — (My future career)
        Includes bibliographical references and index.
        ISBN 0-8368-4241-3 (lib. bdg.)
            1. Child care—Vocational guidance—Juvenile literature.   2. Teaching—
    Vocational guidance—Juvenile literature.   3. Child development—Juvenile
    literature.   4. Vocational guidance—Juvenile literature.   I. Title.
        HQ778.5.M38   2004
        362.71'2'023—dc22   2004045226

This edition first published in 2005 by
Gareth Stevens Publishing
A World Almanac Education Group Company
330 West Olive Street, Suite 100
Milwaukee, Wisconsin 53212 USA

Editor: Dorothy L. Gibbs
Inside design: Peta Morey
Cover design: Melissa Valuch

Picture Credits
Corbis: Jonathan Cavendish 19(b); Corbis cover, 20, 22, 29, 34, 37, 39, 43(l),
51(both), 53, 54, 57, 59(b); Jim Craigmyle 43(r); Laura Dwight 15; Ed Bock
Photography, Inc. 16, 30, 45, 48, 59(t); D. Robert Franz 5; Gaetano 7; Patrik
Giardino 17; Ken Glaser 9; Tom Grill 4, 11(r), 13; Walter Hodges 32; Jeff Zaruba
Studio 19(t); JFPI Studios, Inc. 12, 27(t); John Henley Photography 40, 46; Jose Luis
Pelaez, Inc. 24, 25, 31, 35; Jutta Klee 23; Larry Williams and Associates 27(b), 28,
33, 49; Kevin R. Morris 8; Jules Perrier 6; Steve Prezant 41; Rob Lewine Photography
52; Joel Sartore 11(l); Ariel Skelley 44, 47; Tom Stewart Photography 14, 21, 36, 38,
55, 56.

Gareth Stevens Publishing thanks the following individuals and organizations
for their professional assistance: Nancy Dean, Grandma's House Child Care;
Paul Dupont, PhD, Senior Psychologist, Norris Health Center, University
of Wisconsin – Milwaukee; Carlile L. Schneider, Family Services Manager,
Children's Hospital of Wisconsin; Kristin Bencik Boudreau, D.O., Children's
Medical Group, Bayshore Pediatrics; Pediatric Nurses at Children's Hospital
of Wisconsin; Sandra Bruk, Starms Early Childhood Center.

Printed in China

1 2 3 4 5 6 7 8 9 08 07 06 05 04

Contents

Words that appear in the text in **bold**
type are defined in the glossary.

Child Care Worker

Child care workers look after young children, usually when their parents or guardians are at work or cannot be with them during the day for other reasons. Child care work typically involves infants and preschoolers but may sometimes include even school-age children from five through eleven years old.

A child care worker's job is to provide a **wholesome environment** for young children, keep the children safe and happy, and help them develop some of the skills they will need as they grow older.

A child care worker needs specialized training to take care of infants.

Child care workers are usually employed by day care centers and preschools or nursery schools. They may also work at some hospitals and even in private homes.

Many factories, offices, hotels, shopping malls, and sports or recreation centers have child care facilities, too, so parents can leave their children with qualified caregivers while they are working, shopping, taking classes, or participating in activities of some kind. These facilities are usually run by trained child care workers.

Maria Montessori

Maria Montessori (1870–1952) was Italy's first female physician. From her experiences working with children who had mental disabilities, she developed the Montessori method of education. The Montessori method was based on the belief that young children should be taught in an informal way. Montessori was confident that a child could learn through play and should be allowed to develop at his or her own pace. This method is still the basis of some types of preschool education today.

When looking after children for an entire day, child care workers must provide a variety of activities as well as meals and rest periods. For children who need just a few hours of care, workers mainly supervise activities and help groups of children learn to get along with each other. Child care workers at hotels or shopping malls do not often have contact with the same children on a regular basis, but they still have to provide interesting activities and make sure the children enjoy themselves.

Maria Montessori believed that young children learn directly from their environments.

Providing a safe environment

A child care worker's most important responsibility is to provide a safe environment where children can play and learn. Child care workers must also look after practical needs, such as making sure the children are clean, eat healthy meals, and rest when necessary.

Planning activities

Children learn a lot through play so child care workers must plan and supervise activities that help children develop new skills while having fun. At times, child care workers may plan outside activities, such as walks to parks or visits to libraries or museums, or they may arrange to have visitors come to the school or day care center to teach or entertain the children.

The kinds of skills child care workers most often help children develop include:

- social skills (learning to play with other children and to deal with the world outside their homes)
- practical skills (mastering tasks such as feeding and dressing themselves)

Learning to use a spoon is a big accomplishment for a small child.

Good Points and Bad Points

"The best part of my job is seeing children develop and learn new skills."

"I sometimes get very tired. Young children have a lot of energy and looking after them can be hard work."

Reading to the children is a **fundamental** activity for child care workers.

- creative skills (expressing themselves through drawing, painting, music, and dancing)
- intellectual skills (learning colors, shapes, letters, and numbers)
- emotional skills (becoming more confident and making friends with other children)

Dealing with problems

A child care worker has to get to know every child in his or her group as an individual and needs to be willing and able to help the children with any problems they might face.

Keeping records

Many child care workers are responsible for keeping up-to-date records on all of the children in their care. These records contain information about the child's health and progress in skill development and are often used to guide learning programs for each child.

Main qualifications of a child care worker

Enthusiasm and energy
Child care workers need to be lively and have lots of imaginative ideas for activities that will keep children busy and content.

Gentle firmness
Young children need gentle discipline to help them learn what is right and what is wrong, but even gentle discipline needs to be firmly enforced. Besides being firm, child care workers must also be fair, applying the same rules and guidelines to all children.

Quick thinking
Dangerous situations develop very quickly with young children. A child may suddenly fall, choke on a piece of fruit, or wander away from the group while on a walk. To deal calmly and effectively with these situations, child care workers need to be quick thinkers.

Understanding
Child care workers have to be able to recognize when a child is unhappy or frightened and know how to help children overcome feelings of discomfort.

A trip to a park is an exciting event for toddlers and a chance to learn about flowers, grass, and trees.

First aid training

Accidents happen, no matter how careful and watchful a child care worker might be, so first aid knowledge is essential. Child care workers have to be able to treat cuts and bruises as well as know how to handle children who are choking on food or have swallowed small objects or suddenly become ill.

Playing is an important part of a child's development, physically, socially, and emotionally.

Knowledge of health and safety laws

Laws with regard to health and safety insure that places where children spend time are clean and secure. Child care workers have to know and uphold these laws. Toys and playground equipment, for example, must be safe to use, fire exits must not be blocked, and electrical devices and plumbing equipment must be checked regularly and kept in good condition.

Stephen Lynch

Stephen is a senior child care worker at a day care center.
He works with children who are two and three years old.
The center has two work **shifts**. The early shift is 7:00 a.m.
to 3:45 p.m. The late shift is 9:30 a.m. to 6:15 p.m.

7:00 a.m.   This week, I'm on the early shift so I open up the day care center. I do safety checks to make sure that no cleaning materials have been left out and no furniture or toys are broken. Then I check the telephone messages.

8:00 a.m.   The children start arriving. I play with them to keep them occupied until almost everyone is here.

9:00 a.m.   It's time to clean up. I encourage the children to put toys away after playing with them.

9:30 a.m.   Everyone has a snack of fruit and milk.

9:45 a.m.   The children listen to a story while I change the diapers on children who still wear them. Diapers have to be changed every two hours, and children who are toilet trained must be taken to the bathroom regularly, especially after lunch and naps.

10:00 a.m.   It's time for an art activity. Today, we're looking at pictures of dinosaurs, and the children are making dinosaur models out of cardboard boxes.

11:45 a.m.   Lunchtime.

12:30 p.m.   I clean up the playroom and help get the children settled on mats for a nap. Some sleep for two hours, others for only about twenty minutes. We discuss the children's sleep habits with their parents and try to follow the same routines.

1:00 p.m.   The children who are awake play quietly with toys. I try to keep them from disturbing the children who are still asleep.

2:30 p.m.   Everyone is awake, so we have another snack. Then, after changing diapers and taking children to the bathroom, we all go outside to play.

3:00 p.m.   It's circle time, when we all sit in a circle and talk. Some parents come to pick up their children during this time.

3:45 p.m.   My workday is over. The late shift workers will stay until all the children have gone home.

Spending time outdoors is fun, and it gives the children some fresh air and sunshine.

Young children need a quiet time during the day to sleep or rest.

Child Psychologist

Child **psychologists** are people with highly specialized education and training that qualifies them to help children who have very serious problems. The kinds of problems child psychologists deal with include:

- learning and development problems, such as failure to grow, learn new skills, and keep up with other children of the same age
- behavior and emotional problems, such as unusual habits or frequent misbehavior, that may be due to something that has happened in the child's life to cause feelings of worry, anger, or unhappiness

Some child psychologists work in schools, **clinics**, or hospitals. Others are self-employed and have **private practices** through which they provide direct assistance to individuals and families or serve as **consultants** to various organizations and groups.

A child psychologist often works directly with a child, meeting the child for regularly scheduled, one-on-one sessions. A child psychologist may also work indirectly, first, meeting with a child for one or more

Keeping up with new research is an important part of a child psychologist's responsibilities.

Looking at How Children Learn

Besides working just with children who have problems, some child psychologists try to help all children. They may do research, for example, into how children learn. The results of their research are often used to develop teaching materials.

Over the years, child psychologists have discovered a lot about how children learn to read. This knowledge has led to the development of different ways to teach children to read.

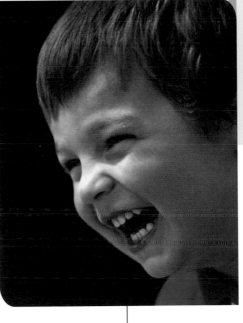

assessment sessions to determine what is wrong, then working with parents or professionals, such as doctors, teachers, child care workers, or **social workers**, to develop support programs. Dealing with a child who does not like school and is often absent, a child psychologist might try to encourage more frequent attendance by making arrangements for the child to be in school only a short period of time each day. By maintaining regular contact with a teacher or a caregiver to discuss the child's progress, the psychologist can adjust the program as needed.

To be able to help children deal with their problems and difficulties, a child psychologist has to be very interested in how the human mind works as well as in how children develop.

To achieve the best results, child psychologists usually try to make the time they spend with children fun.

Main responsibilities of a child psychologist

To help a child, a psychologist has to get to know the child and identify the child's problems. A psychologist gets to know a child in the following ways:

- spending a lot of time talking to the child and listening carefully to what the child says
- talking to parents and other adults who know the child well, to learn about the child's background and to discover possible causes for problems
- watching the child play with toys and with other children, both at school or a day care center and at home (Watching a child play lets a psychologist see, first hand, how the child behaves and what skills the child has.)
- giving the child tasks or tests that help measure what he or she can and cannot do

A psychologist can learn a lot about a child by just sitting down and talking with the child.

Good Points and Bad Points

"Working with other people to help children overcome problems is very rewarding. There are times, however, when I see my advice ignored, and this is frustrating."

Special kinds of tests help child psychologists discover how children think and solve problems.

After getting to know a child and his or her problems, the child psychologist's main responsibility is developing a program to help the child.

Children who often become violent when they are angry may benefit from anger management programs. These programs try to help children understand what causes their anger and learn how to deal with the feelings before they explode into a **tantrum**. An anger management program may also involve training adults to recognize early signs of incidents and help children cope without violence.

The responsibilities of a child psychologist include sharing information with parents, caregivers, and other adults who may be involved in making decisions to help the child and giving advice on how best to provide help. A child psychologist's recommendations might include:

- extra support at school or in day care
- individual or group **therapy** sessions
- placement in a facility run by specially trained staff

Because work with a child can go on for several years, the child psychologist must conduct regular reviews to **monitor** progress and to determine whether the kind of help the child is receiving is still appropriate.

Main qualifications of a child psychologist

Observation skills
To understand what is troubling a child, a psychologist has to be very observant and able to pick up on even the smallest clues.

Analytical ability
An important part of a child psychologist's work involves examining notes and reports about a child's background and behavior and analyzing the information to determine the best ways to help the child.

Adaptability
All children are different so child psychologists must be able to adapt the ways they work to best meet the needs of each child. They must also be able to find different ways to help different children.

Watching a child play tells a child psychologist a lot about the child's behavior and skills.

Patience
Helping children understand and cope with their problems can be a slow process. Child psychologists must have a lot of patience, especially during long periods of time when a child does not seem to be making much progress.

Emotional strength
Working with children who are struggling with difficult problems can be distressing and heartbreaking. Child psychologists must be able to cope with sad situations.

Keeping detailed written records and reports is an important part of the job for child psychologists.

Communication skills

Child psychologists must be friendly and able to put children at ease. They must also be able to explain things clearly to children and their parents and to any other adults involved in the children's care and support.

Teamwork

To make their support programs successful, child psychologists must enjoy working with all kinds of caregivers, including parents, teachers, and doctors.

Organization skills

The paperwork alone demands good organization skills.

fact file

The requirements to qualify for professional training in child psychology include a bachelor's degree, followed by a graduate degree in psychology, usually at the doctoral level.

Most school psychologists, who work with children in public and private schools, will have earned degrees in programs specializing in education and psychology. A two- or three-year postgraduate degree in school psychology is usually needed to get state certification or a license to work as a school psychologist.

Fiona McKendrick

Fiona is a child psychologist who works at a center to which children are referred by other professionals who have recognized growth or development problems. Fiona has a bachelor's degree in sociology and psychology and a master's degree in clinical psychology.

8:45 a.m. The day begins with a team meeting, during which our staff psychologists discuss the children who have appointments that day.

9:30 a.m. I spend the next two hours in our center's assessment nursery, where preschool children come for sessions with one or two other children so the staff can observe them while they play.

I play with the children, observing their skills and behaviors, and I find out information about the children from their parents and caregivers.

12:00 p.m. I attend a feedback session with parents to discuss my observations in the assessment nursery, but any decisions about a child's future are made in a discussion with other professionals.

12:45 p.m. I leave the center for a home visit with a child who has eating problems. I want to make sure I'm there at a mealtime. I talk with the child's mother about ways to encourage the child to eat.

2:15 p.m. Back at the center, I conduct a family therapy session designed to provide social skills training for an autistic child. Autism is a development disorder that affects an individual's social and communication skills and his or her imagination.

3:45 p.m.   I leave the center, again, for a school visit to talk over reports on a couple of students with their teachers and to discuss ways to help the students deal with their difficulties.

5:00 p.m.   It's time to head home, but I take some paper-work with me to go over during the evening.

Child psychologists frequently exchange ideas and information with other professionals.

Seeing children learning to overcome their problems can be very rewarding.

Child Therapist

What is a child therapist?

Child **therapists** use different kinds of activities to help children overcome physical and emotional problems and cope with disabilities. They work with children both one-on-one and in groups of children who have similar problems. They work in hospitals, clinics, schools, day care centers, and other health and educational facilities. Some even visit children at home. Therapists who are self-employed may work for many organizations.

Some child therapists specialize in helping children overcome particular problems caused by ill health, physical or mental disabilities, accidents, or medical treatments. Three examples of these kinds of therapists are:

- speech therapists (work with children who have speech and language difficulties due to either physical problems, such as hearing loss or the way their mouths and tongues are formed, or emotional problems)
- physical therapists (help children develop the use and control of their arms, legs, and other parts of their bodies or regain physical movement after some kind of **trauma**, such as an accident or an operation)

Making sure a child's limbs are exercised properly is very important after an accident or operation.

- child psychotherapists (help children learn how to express their feelings in healthy ways and how to cope with difficult events in their lives)

Most children have trouble understanding unpleasant events, such as divorce or the death of a parent or **sibling**. Faced with situations like these, children are often too confused or worried to talk to adults about what is wrong and how they feel.

Many types of **therapies** and methods use enjoyable or artistic activities to help children deal with various kinds of emotional distress. Play therapy, for example, uses games and other playtime activities to help children learn to express themselves or to teach them effective ways to cope with feelings such as confusion, anger, grief, and sadness. Much the same way play therapy uses games, other therapies use activities in music, art, or drama.

Playing a musical instrument is fun, but it can also be a way to handle difficult events or painful emotions.

Main responsibilities of a child therapist

Some children need therapy for just a short time to help them cope with an operation or a stay in the hospital. Children who have experienced a tragedy, such as the loss of a parent, or are deeply troubled by a serious problem may need therapy for months or even years. In either case, child therapists help children in many different ways.

Whatever the type of therapy, child therapists use their skills to help children individually. When therapists are working with groups of children, they still have to be aware of the individual needs of each child. How child therapists work varies tremendously, and there is no one "right" way.

Many kinds of therapists use dolls and other toys in therapeutic play to help children understand their problems. In hospitals, toy medical equipment is often used to calm worried children and to explain what is going to happen so the real thing will be less frightening.

Working well with others is an important goal of many of the activities used in drama therapy.

Good Points and Bad Points

"Music activities are great fun, and I enjoy seeing the children being creative. Being a therapist, however, requires a lot of patience because it takes a long time to win someone's trust."

Drama therapists use acting activities to help children

- learn to work and play as part of a group
- develop imagination and creative abilities
- gain confidence and view themselves in positive ways.

Music therapists encourage children to:

- enjoy music, including singing and using instruments and objects to make music.
- use music to help them relax and deal with serious problems and difficult situations.

Art therapists use arts and crafts activities, such as model making, sculpting clay, drawing, or painting. Art can be a way to express many feelings that are often too difficult for children to understand or put into words.

In art therapy, a painting activity can often help a child express fear, pain, or sadness.

Main qualifications of a child therapist

Background in health or social sciences
Child therapists come from a variety of educational backgrounds and work experience, but most of them have college degrees in psychology, sociology, or **social work**.

Energy and enthusiasm
To encourage children to participate in activities and enjoy themselves, a child therapist needs a lot of energy, both physical and emotional. Therapists also need to show a lot of enthusiasm for their work.

Imagination
Because no two children are exactly the same, no single program or activity will meet every child's needs. Child therapists have to be imaginative and able to develop a variety of programs and activities. They also have to be able to adapt programs to suit individual children.

Progress is often slow, and the work can be very demanding, so child therapists must have a lot of patience.

Listening skills
Before therapists can help children with their problems, they have to get to know each child as an individual. Therapists learn a lot about children simply by listening to what they say. Good listening skills, therefore, are extremely important. Observing how a child behaves is equally important, however, because children cannot or will not always tell a therapist everything the therapist needs to know.

Emotional strength

Coming to terms with their problems can be very difficult for children. Child therapists need tremendous emotional strength to cope, day after day, with children who are angry, frightened, or sad.

Organization skills

Child therapists usually have busy schedules that often include professional meetings and travel as well as appointments. All of these activities also mean a lot of paperwork. To keep schedules on track and records up to date, therapists must be well organized.

fact file

To be licensed to practice, a physical therapist or a speech therapist must have a master's degree from an accredited college or university. The requirements for the degree will have included both course work and supervised practice with patients in hospitals, clinics, or schools.

The requirements for training in music, art, drama, or play therapy usually include at least a bachelor's degree, or similar education, in a related field, plus work experience helping children or adults.

An art therapist makes creative activities, such as paper cutouts, both entertaining and healing.

A day in the life of a child therapist

Carol Lowery

Carol is a Certified Child Life Specialist and has a master's degree in Child Life. She works at a children's hospital on an **orthopedic** unit.

8:30 a.m. I attend a weekly meeting to review all patients on the unit. I discuss what patient needs I have observed and explain what I have been working on with patients and their families.

9:00 a.m. I walk through the unit, stopping to see all of the patients and their visitors, to help me determine what services I need to provide today.

9:30 a.m. I open the activity room on the unit and ask my morning volunteer to take some activities to patients who have to stay in their rooms. We offer all kinds of toys and creative arts activities for a variety of ages, from infants through teens.

11:30 a.m. The patients are back in their rooms for lunch so I clean up the activity room and grab a bite to eat.

12:30 p.m. I meet with a patient for a preadmission visit before his surgery. I show the patient and his parents photographs, and we talk about what will happen on the day of the surgery. He plays with hospital equipment, then we take a short tour. I give him a doctor's hat and mask and a special surgical doll to take home and practice doing surgery on.

1:45 p.m. I talk to a group of new nurses about using play to communicate with children. I stress that every child must be treated as an individual.

2:15 p.m. I visit patients who must stay in bed.

3:00 p.m.   A nurse asks me to help a patient through a painful medical treatment. I use books, music, and special toys to distract the patient during the procedure.

3:30 p.m.   I continue my bedside visits.

4:15 p.m.   I make notes in their medical records about what I did with patients today and how they responded.

Therapeutic play in a hospital can include all kinds of fun activities.

Child therapists can take a lot of the fear out of having to stay in a hospital.

Pediatrician

What is a pediatrician?

Pediatricians are medical doctors who specialize in the care of children from birth to about age eighteen. Children are usually examined by a pediatrician right after they are born. As they grow up, most children visit pediatricians regularly for health and development checkups and to be **immunized** against serious diseases, such as measles, mumps, **diphtheria**, and **polio**.

Most pediatricians work in **private practices**, which means that they are self-employed and have their own offices, often in medical centers, where they see patients who typically have scheduled appointments. Besides seeing patients at their offices, pediatricians often treat patients at one or more hospitals, and some may even visit patients at their homes.

All children need regular medical care, especially babies, whose early stages of development need frequent **monitoring**.

Along with providing regular checkups and preventative care, pediatricians treat children for routine illnesses, such as colds, sore throats, and ear infections. They also provide emergency care to patients who contract serious illnesses or are injured in accidents.

When children's medical needs require hospitalization, their pediatricians take care of them in one of the following ways:

A World Health Success Story

Pediatricians are concerned with maintaining high health standards, not just for their own patients but for all children. A big success in the history of child health was ending **smallpox** around the world. In 1967, the **World Health Organization** started a campaign to **vaccinate** all children against smallpox. The last recorded case of the disease was in 1978.

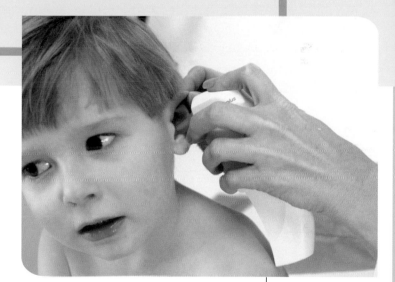

An ear infection is a common childhood **ailment** that often requires a visit to a pediatrician.

- As **outpatients**, children are in the hospital for scheduled medical treatments, minor surgeries, or emergency care, but they do not stay overnight.
- As **inpatients**, children remain in the hospital for a full day or more to receive ongoing treatments that require careful supervision or to have major surgery.

Pediatricians often visit young inpatients daily, either to perform treatments or to monitor their progress.

Main responsibilities of a pediatrician

Much of a pediatrician's work is the same as any other medical doctor's. It involves taking care of the general health of patients. The difference is that pediatricians' patients are all children.

Normal growth and development generally means that a child is in good health. Problems in either area are usually signs that there is something wrong. Children need to visit their pediatricians regularly, throughout childhood, for check-ups. A routine checkup usually includes the following:

- measuring height and weight
- testing hearing and vision
- checking speech development

Besides looking for physical problems, most pediatricians also look for behavioral and emotional problems at a child's checkup.

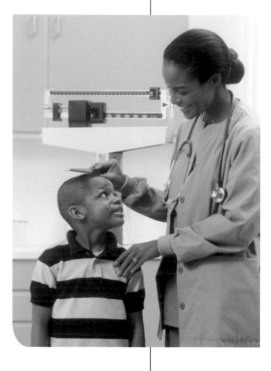

A pediatrician measures and weighs a child at each checkup to make sure the child is at the right levels for his or her age.

Good Points and Bad Points

"The best part of being a pediatrician is seeing children recover and enjoy life again."

"Treating a child who is ill or in pain can be very difficult. Dealing with worried and upset parents and relatives is also hard."

In addition to regular checkups, pediatricians provide many other medical services, including:

Pediatricians visit their patients who are in the hospital almost daily, even if it's just to say hello.

- immunizations (When children reach certain ages, pediatricians immunize them against diseases such as measles and polio so they will not catch them later in life when the effects are often more harmful. Immunizations can be either **injections** of a vaccine or a vaccine that is taken by mouth.)
- **diagnosis** and treatment of common ailments, such as colds and flu, and childhood diseases, such as mumps and chicken pox
- treatments for cuts, **sprains**, and **fractures**, usually caused by childhood activities such as falling off of bicycles and out of trees
- coordination of hospital care with nurses, physical **therapists**, **radiologists**, and other health care workers

Main qualifications of a pediatrician

Premed education
A bachelor's degree in an accredited premed program
is an essential **prerequisite** for medical school.

Observation skills
Babies and young children cannot explain how they feel
or where they hurt, which can make diagnosing their
problems difficult. Pediatricians have to get to know
their patients well and be able to spot even the smallest
changes in their health or development.

Patience and a gentle touch
Even healthy children are often frightened by doctors
and easily become upset. A pediatrician must be patient
and reassuring to comfort a child and win his or her
confidence. Performing examinations and treatments
slowly and carefully is important. Pediatricians need
a gentle but sure
touch so children
experience as little
pain or discomfort
as possible.

To provide good
medical care to
young patients,
pediatricians
have to get to
know parents
and other care-
givers as well
as the children
themselves.

Emotional strength
Taking care of sick
and injured children
can be very hard,
and pediatricians
must also face the
harsh reality that
not every patient
gets better. Pediatricians must have tremendous
emotional strength, especially when dealing with
children who are critically ill or in great pain.

Patients' records must be kept up to date and easily accessible.

Communication skills

Pediatricians must be able to give instructions and explain complicated scientific and medical information clearly and in a way that can be easily understood, even by people who do not have a lot of medical knowledge.

Teamwork

Keeping children healthy and making sick or injured children well involves more than just the patient and the doctor. A pediatrician must work as part of a team that includes both medical and nonmedical caregivers.

fact file

Pediatricians are trained first as doctors, which means four years of medical school followed by a one-year **internship**. After general training, doctors complete a minimum of three years of **pediatric** training, which usually requires a pediatric **residency**, before they can be certified as pediatric specialists.

Kristin Bencik Boudreau

Kristin is a pediatrician who has a private practice within a children's medical group.

7:30 a.m.   I get my two-year-old up and ready for the day. Many pediatricians are mommies or daddies, too.

8:30 a.m.   I go to one or more hospitals to see my patients. The visits can involve anything from checking on a newborn to arranging an admission for a sick child. After seeing a patient, I always update his or her parents as well as any other physicians that might be helping with the patient's care.

10:00 a.m. I start seeing patients at my office. Many of my appointments are routine checkups for healthy children. A checkup is basically a physical exam that includes measuring height, weight, and, on babies, head **circumference**. I mark all of a patient's measurements on a growth chart so parents can see how their child is developing.

Besides providing a full physical exam, I assess how well the child's speech, **motor**, and social skills are developing. I also talk to the child and his or her parents about how to prevent injuries.

12:00 p.m. Lunchtime is usually catch-up time, too.

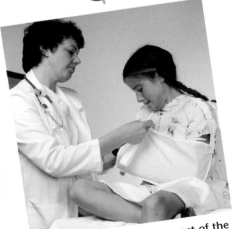

Treating patients can take most of the day and, sometimes, most of the night.

X rays are important medical tools for treating injuries such as broken bones.

I make phone calls, look through paperwork, and try to update the patients' charts from my morning appointments.

1:00 p.m. I continue seeing patients. Along with physical exams, I also have sick visits, which range from colds and ear infections to sprains and fractures. Occasionally, I see a child who is sick enough to have to send to a hospital for treatment.

5:00 p.m. I finish making phone calls, doing paperwork, and updating charts. Once a week, a pediatric resident, or pediatrician in training, spends the afternoon with me. I discuss my patients with the resident to help teach him or her how to be a pediatrician.

6:30 p.m. I go home to make dinner and become a mommy again. If I am on call, I will take care of patients throughout the night.

Pediatric Nurse

What is a pediatric nurse?

Pediatric nurses are **registered nurses** who have additional education and training in medical nursing care for children from birth to about age eighteen.

They work in doctor's offices, **clinics**, hospitals, and schools. Some work in **intensive care** units, nursing children who are very seriously ill. Others care for sick children in **hospices**. These children are too ill to recover, but hospice nurses do their best to keep the children as comfortable and free of pain as possible. Many pediatric nurses work in the community, advising parents and caregivers on how to look after sick children and, sometimes, even caring for sick children at home.

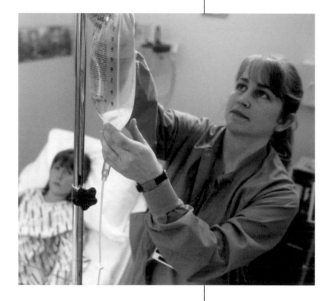

In hospitals, pediatric nurses provide ongoing medical care, which includes making sure that children get the right kinds of medicines in the right amounts.

Children, especially when they are very young, can develop illnesses quickly and can become extremely sick. Furthermore, some illnesses, such as **croup** and chickenpox, are more likely to affect children than adults. Treating children's illnesses and other childhood health conditions requires specialized knowledge and training. Pediatric nurses have the skills and experience to deal with the special medical needs of children.

Keeping Kids Healthy

Pediatric nurses, especially those working in the community, help educate the public on a variety of children's health and safety issues, from **asthma** control to babysitter training. They often play leading roles in **outreach programs** offered through many hospitals and medical centers. These programs provide classes, workshops, hands-on learning, publications, field trips, and health care events that teach preventative care to keep kids healthy.

Most pediatric nurses care mainly for children who are sick or injured, but many work with children who have physical or mental disabilities.

Having nurses who specialize in the care of children is extremely important because, unlike adults' bodies, children's bodies are still growing and developing. When their growth or development is affected by illness or injury, children need the expert help of pediatricians and pediatric nurses. To specialize in pediatric care, a nurse has to be very interested in child health and must keep up to date with all the changes and new developments in pediatric medicine.

When children are hospitalized, pediatric nurses help them get settled and try to keep them comfortable.

Main responsibilities of a pediatric nurse

Pediatric nurses work very closely with other medical professionals, including doctors and **therapists**. They also work very closely with patients. Having so much contact with their young patients, especially those who are hospitalized, pediatric nurses play a key role in patient recovery and return to health.

One of the main responsibilities of pediatric nurses is to comfort young patients and help them understand, as far as possible, what is happening to them.

Patients rely on pediatric nurses for information and support as well as for actual medical care.

Most adult patients are able to understand their medical problems and treatments, but children, especially the very young, have little, if any, idea what is happening to them or why. Children are often frightened by the treatments they receive, so pediatric nurses must always try to work calmly and carefully.

Good Points and Bad Points

"Helping children get well is truly rewarding."

"The most difficult part of my job is accepting that not all of my patients will recover."

The work of a pediatric nurse includes:

Until a wound heals, dressings and bandages must be changed regularly.

- checking patient's **vital signs**
- measuring height and weight
- giving patients medicines and **injections**
- cleaning wounds and changing **dressings** and bandages
- taking out stitches after wounds have healed
- drawing blood from patients and sending blood tests to laboratories to be analyzed
- keeping detailed files, records, and charts of patient information, including their health conditions, treatments, and progress
- getting to know patients, entertaining them and playing with them, providing emotional support, and, for those who are old enough to understand, explaining what is happening to them
- discussing patients' progress with their relatives and caregivers and helping relatives and caregivers cope with any distress they feel

Main qualifications of a pediatric nurse

Strong interest in children's health

Pediatric nursing requires background and interest in sciences that are related to preventing diseases and promoting good health, especially children's health.

Positive attitude

Having a positive attitude and outlook is extremely important. Pediatric nurses deal with many sad and distressing cases. They have to be strong enough to take care of patients' medical needs while, at the same time, providing emotional support to the patients and their families.

Tact

To win the confidence of patients and family members, pediatric nurses must be sensitive and reassuring. When children are sick or hurt, the nurses caring for them play a big part in helping everyone cope.

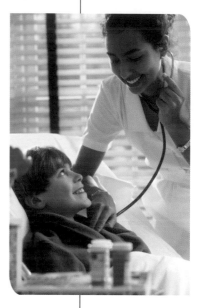

Calm approach and a strong stomach

Children often have medical emergencies. Whether they are illnesses or injuries, emergencies must be dealt with quickly and efficiently. A cool head and a calm approach are vital. To deal with blood, vomit, and other messiness that accompanies injuries and illnesses, pediatric nurses also need to have strong stomachs.

To children who are hospitalized, pediatric nurses often become special friends.

Good hands and a gentle touch

Some medical treatments are very difficult to perform on babies and small children. To cause young patients as little pain and discomfort as possible, pediatric nurses have to be good with their hands and very gentle.

Pediatric nurses work in **shifts** to provide care all day and all night.

fact file

Pediatric nurses must first graduate from an accredited nursing program, earning a diploma, an associate's degree, or a bachelor's degree. Then, they pursue further training, which includes working with sick children under the guidance and supervision of qualified pediatricians, pediatric nurses, and pediatric specialists.

Communication skills

Speaking and writing skills are essential in pediatric nursing. Nurses have to provide clear information and instructions to patients and their families as well as to other medical professionals. They also have to write reports on patients' treatments and progress.

A day in the life of a pediatric nurse

Ben Stevens

Ben is a pediatric nurse running a pediatric surgical ward. He works a four-day week, involving two twelve-and-a-half-hour clinic days, spent on the ward, and two eight-hour office days, dealing with paperwork.

7:30 a.m.   It's a clinical day, and I arrive on the ward.

7:45 a.m.   First, night staff members **brief** the day staff on events that occurred during their shift. Then, I assign patients to nurses, and each nurse gets bedside updates from the night nurses caring for his or her patients.

8:00 a.m.   I go around the ward checking patients' charts and medications and talking to parents. Many parents or caregivers stay on the ward with their children overnight.

8:45 a.m.   The ward has four resident pediatricians. I try to accompany them on their rounds, and I provide information when a patient's nurse is not available.

10:00 a.m.   I organize morning breaks, arranging for staff to cover for nurses assigned to patients who need constant care.

10:30 a.m.   I do rounds, again. Throughout the day, physical therapists, **dieticians**, and other medical staff visit patients, and I update them on the progress each patient is making.

12:00 p.m.   One afternoon a week, I attend a bed meeting, during which medical staff discuss patients who will be coming in the following week.

On another afternoon, I attend a meeting with **social workers** and play therapists to discuss the social needs of patients and their families.

4:00 p.m. When there's a quiet time of day, it's usually about now.

5:00 p.m. I accompany pediatricians on evening rounds.

7:00 p.m. To prepare for the arrival of the night staff, I update and print out patient handover sheets.

7:45 p.m. When the handover from day staff to night staff has been completed, it's time to go home.

Each patient's treatments and progress need to be recorded in careful detail.

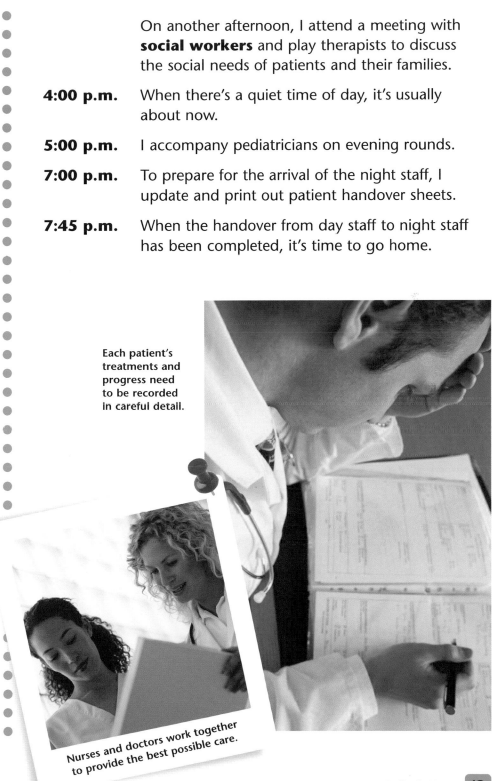

Nurses and doctors work together to provide the best possible care.

Preschool Teacher

What is a preschool teacher?

Preschool teachers, who may also be known as nursery school teachers, work with children who are not yet old enough to start formal schooling but are ready to explore the world in a more social setting and, guided by their teachers, begin to learn new skills that will prepare them for formal schooling.

These teachers work in day care centers as well as in preschools and nursery schools, and some programs are even run in home settings. Preschool education may be provided at no charge by public school systems or other government-funded organizations. Other preschools are privately run, so parents must pay fees for their children to attend.

Preschool teachers know how to make learning fun.

Preschools provide safe, stimulating **environments** in which children can participate in a variety of learning experiences. In some programs, preschool staff decide topics of study, then link activities to different themes, such as the zoo, the farm, families, or holidays. Other preschool programs are more child-directed, and topics of study depend more on the interests children express.

The First Nursery School

In 1926, German educator Friedrich Froebel (1782–1852) wrote the book *On the Education of Man*, in which he set out his ideas about teaching through play. Froebel believed that children as young as age three were capable of learning. In 1836, he opened the first nursery school, or *kindergarten* ("garden of children"). He trained teachers in his school so they could open other nursery schools based on his ideas.

Children usually enter preschool in the year or year and a half before they will begin formal schooling. By this age, most children have some social skills, and they are able to talk and can feed and dress themselves. Because the children are still very young, however, they usually have difficulty doing a directed activity for very long.

Art is a good way for young children to express their ideas and to represent their worth.

Preschool teaching, therefore, is mostly informal and done mainly through play. To learn numbers and how to count, for example, children might build towers with blocks, then count the number of blocks they used.

Main responsibilities of a preschool teacher

A preschool teacher's main responsibilities include:

- guiding children to becoming capable learners and having confidence in themselves as learners
- helping children enjoy learning
- teaching children how to function successfully in a classroom setting

Teachers and other preschool staff work as a team to create enjoyable and effective learning programs.

Good Points and Bad Points

"The children I teach are at a wonderful age, and I enjoy being with them very much."

"My job is hectic, and I often find that I run out of time for all the things I have to do."

- getting to know each child as an individual and creating learning programs based on each child's age and abilities

Meeting these responsibilities involves the following kinds of tasks:

- designing and preparing learning activities and teaching materials, such as simple games, puzzles, name cards, and picture cards
- arranging field trips to places such as the public library or a museum, as well as arranging for visitors, such as members of police or fire departments, to come talk to the children about safety rules and how they do their jobs
- measuring each child's progress and keeping records to show his or her development
- communicating with parents and other caregivers to form a strong link between home and school
- working with schoolteachers, **psychologists**, speech **therapists**, and other professionals to make sure the children are healthy, happy, and progressing normally

Main qualifications of a preschool teacher

A strong interest in early childhood education

Teaching preschool requires not only a love of children and concern for their welfare but also a commitment to early childhood education and learning through play.

Friendliness

For children to feel comfortable with them, preschool teachers need to be friendly and cheerful. Children who are worried or frightened by a teacher usually find learning difficult.

Discipline

Rules and discipline are needed to create an atmosphere in which children feel secure and are able to learn. The discipline should be firm but always kind and gentle.

Enthusiasm and creativity

To make learning fun, preschool teachers have to be lively and show a lot of enthusiasm for their work, and they have to plan activities that are both enjoyable and interesting.

Communication skills

Good communication is very important. Preschool teachers have to make information and explanations clear and easy to understand, whether they are communicating with a child, a child's parents or caregivers, another member of the preschool staff, or other child care professionals. When discussing problems or difficulties with a child's parents or caregivers, tact is important, too.

A preschool teacher has to develop good relationships with both the children and their parents or caregivers.

Encouragement and praise from their preschool teachers help children start to enjoy learning.

fact file

To qualify for jobs, preschool teachers have to complete six semester units of course work in early childhood education. Once they have jobs, they must complete six more units.

Quick thinking

To effectively handle accidents, sudden illnesses, **tantrums**, fights, and other unexpected situations, a preschool teacher has to be able to think and act quickly and competently.

Organization skills

To be effective, the preschool environment must be well thought out and organized. Also, teachers have to keep a lot of paperwork and school records organized.

Claire Aylward

Claire is a preschool teacher in a private nursery school. She has a degree in psychology and teaching certification in early childhood education.

8:15 a.m.   After a quick **briefing** with other staff members, I start greeting the children as they arrive.

8:30 a.m.   Fruit and drinks are set out for a snack, and the children take turns serving each other and passing out cups and napkins.

9:00 a.m.   We sing some songs, then read and talk about our daily topic. Today, we read about farming, and the children decide to turn the sandbox into a farm with plastic animals, a tractor, and "fields."

I make notes on their comments and questions to help me remember what they know and what they are wondering about.

9:30 a.m.   The children have free playtime to explore materials on their own. The materials are set up in specific areas, such as housekeeping, art, and library corner. Teachers play alongside the children, encouraging them to try new ideas and use their skills.

10:45 a.m.   We have a daily math lesson and follow the same learning-to-read program as the schools the children will be attending, but most learning is through playful activities with direct help from teachers and other staff members. The children can choose the activities they want to do and are allowed to move from one activity to another.

11:15 a.m.   Unless it's raining, we go outside to play games.

11:45 a.m. Lunchtime.

12:15 p.m. Now, it's rest time. We play soft music and read stories. After twenty minutes, the children who are not asleep can play quietly.

1:15 p.m. As the children wake up, they have a snack and enjoy some free play activities.

2:30 p.m. We do more teacher-led activities, such as planting seeds and playing matching and sorting games.

3:00 p.m. With the day winding down, the children either do quiet tabletop activities or listen to stories.

4:00 p.m. All of the children have gone home by now so the staff has a chance to talk over the day's events and prepare for tomorrow's activities.

Learning numbers can be easy when they are part of a game.

Young children can develop a number of skills by playing musical instruments.

Schoolteacher

What is a schoolteacher?

Schoolteachers are responsible for educating children. With very young children, their main task is teaching the basic skills of reading, writing, and working with numbers. Along with these basic skills, they may also teach other subjects, such as geography and science.

A schoolteacher may have to teach fifteen to thirty students at the same time.

Exams Are Nothing New

Exams have been around for a very long time. In ancient China, for example, people who wanted to work in certain government jobs had to take examinations designed to test their knowledge of Chinese literature. Those who earned the highest marks, or grades, on these examinations got the jobs.

Most schoolteachers work with children of a particular age group. The age groups are typically as follows:

- elementary school — 6 to 10 years
- middle school — 11 to 14 years
- high school — 15 to 18 years

Elementary schoolteachers, who work with children up to about eleven years old, are, most often, classroom teachers. These teachers have the same class, or group of children, for almost all of their lessons, and they teach most, if not all, of the lessons in the same classroom.

Working in a group can be a very good way to learn.

When children move on to middle school and high school, the teaching system changes. These age groups normally have specialist teachers and move throughout the school, from one room to another, for each class. Most specialist teachers are responsible for lessons in only one or two subjects. Which subjects they teach depends on their educational background and prior teaching or work experience.

Main responsibilities of a schoolteacher

Schoolteachers spend most of each school day in the classroom, giving lessons to students. These lessons, however, don't just happen. Teachers spend a lot of time planning them. They want to make sure that the lessons are interesting and that all of the students in the class are given work to match their levels of ability.

In addition to educating his or her students, a schoolteacher plays a caring role. When students have problems, teachers are there to help.

Along with planning and giving lessons, teachers' responsibilities include:

- reviewing, grading, and commenting on students' schoolwork (which helps teachers know what students do or do not understand and helps encourage students to do well in their studies)
- discussing progress with students and helping them with any problems they are having
- recording students' achievements and progress and sending written reports to parents and caregivers

Good Points and Bad Points

"I love being with the children and planning and teaching classes, but paperwork can be a problem. There are always forms to fill out and reports to prepare, and with all my teaching work, I find it very difficult to get the paperwork done."

- keeping up with new information and developments in the subjects they teach as well as with changes in the way lessons are taught and schools are run

It might seem as if the hours teachers work are short, but their time spent in the classroom is only part of the work. Most teachers put in many hours a week outside the classroom, preparing lessons, writing and designing work sheets, grading homework, and keeping up with all of the record keeping.

Schools organize regular meetings between teachers and parents or caregivers so that school and home can work together in helping students succeed academically. These meetings are usually held after school hours, often in the evenings, but teachers always try to make themselves available to parents and caregivers who want to discuss their students' educational progress.

Many teachers also spend after school or evening hours involved in **extracurricular** activities and clubs related to sports, music, art, drama, careers, and other areas of interest to students. Teachers often have duties even during lunch and breaks, when they may be responsible for keeping an eye on students' behavior.

Outside the classroom, schoolteachers often spend many hours coaching sports teams or supervising other school-sponsored clubs and activities.

Main qualifications of a schoolteacher

Respect for children
Teaching children requires respect for them, whatever their backgrounds or abilities. Schoolteachers must also be able to treat all students fairly.

Communication skills
Schoolteachers need not only a good understanding of the subjects they teach but also the ability to explain the subject matter to students in a way that is interesting, clear, and easy to understand.

Liveliness
Students learn best when they find lessons exciting as well as informative.

Patience
Educating a class of children with a wide range of ideas and abilities demands a great deal of patience.

Discipline
To be able to concentrate on their schoolwork, students must have a proper classroom atmosphere. Teachers need to adopt a fair but firm approach to discipline to make sure all students behave appropriately at all times.

Schoolteachers must find ways to make lessons interesting and plan activities that allow their students to learn by doing.

Teamwork
Schoolteachers have to like people of all ages and be able to get along with them. They also have to like working as part of a team. A teacher's team typically includes other teachers, parents and caregivers, school administrators, and, most importantly, students.

Talking over a
difficult problem
with a teacher
is often the first
step to solving it.

fact file

Being a teacher requires a
a college or university degree
in an education program that
includes a teaching qualification.
Alternatively, you can earn a
degree in any subject, then
take teacher training courses
to obtain teaching credentials.

Organization skills

To manage their busy working
lives, schoolteachers need to
be very well organized, both
in and away from school.
Teaching requires a lot of
paperwork, from lesson plans
and progress reports to exams
and worksheets. Teachers also
have to keep track of many appointments and meetings.
Regular meetings with other staff members as well as
with parents and caregivers are all part of the job and
must be carefully coordinated with lesson planning and
teaching responsibilities.

A day in the life of a schoolteacher

Phil Grainger

Phil teaches history classes at a large, four-year high school.

8:15 a.m. As soon as I arrive, I check my E-mails for news and information about students, lesson changes, meetings, and special events.

8:45 a.m. I take attendance in my **homeroom** class of thirteen- and fourteen-year-olds. After we go over the day's activities, I collect notes from parents, pass on messages and announcements, and try to help students who are having problems.

9:05 a.m. I teach two classes of fourteen-year-olds about ancient Greece. We're looking at aspects of everyday life for the ancient Greeks. Topics of discussion include housing, food, education, medicine, and leisure activities.

10:35 a.m. It's break time. I usually manage to have a cup of coffee, but I often spend this time catching up on work from previous classes.

10:55 a.m. I'm back in my homeroom, where the class is writing comments about their report cards. I encourage them to focus on developing their strengths and understanding their weaknesses.

11:40 a.m. I teach a class of sixteen-year-olds who are working on projects related to World War II. I check on their progress and answer any questions they might have.

12:25 p.m. I help a class of eighteen-year-olds prepare for examinations on the Russian Revolution and the history of the United States.

1:10 p.m. Lunchtime is only forty-five minutes. I eat quickly while I work on transportation arrangements for next week's field trip.

1:55 p.m. I work with a group of students who are having difficulties with their schoolwork. We may work on history, or I might help them with reading and writing skills.

3:25 p.m. The school day is over, but my workday is not. I have worksheets to prepare and plenty of papers to grade before tomorrow's classes.

When the lesson is interesting, students are eager to participate.

Time after classes have ended for the day is time to tackle the paperwork.

Glossary

ailment – an illness, disease, or some other physical discomfort

assessment – evaluation or appraisal

asthma – a type of allergy that can cause coughing, gasping, and difficulty breathing

brief – (v) to provide information or instructions

circumference – the distance around the outside of a circular object

clinics – medical centers where doctors and other medical staff diagnose and treat ailments on an outpatient basis

consultants – experts in a profession who provide advice and services on a contract basis for a fee

croup – inflammation of the throat and windpipe, usually in children, causing severe coughing and difficulty breathing

diagnosis – the identification of an illness through the evaluation of a patient's signs and symptoms

dieticians – specialists in the uses of food and nutrition for good health

diphtheria – a serious, contagious disease that causes inflammation of the heart and nervous system

dressings – materials, such as gauze and ointments, that are used to cover a wound

environment – the surroundings of an area or lifestyle, including the physical, social, and cultural conditions

extracurricular – beyond or outside of the normal hours of a school day

fractures – broken bones

fundamental – basic or essential

homeroom – the classroom in which a group of students starts each school day

hospices – hospitals for patients who have incurable illnesses

immunized – introduced a virus or some other substance into the body, either by injection or by mouth, to help the body resist a contagious or deadly disease

injections – medicines or nutrients forced into the body through needles

inpatients – patients who must stay in a hospital, day and night over a period of time, to receive medical care

intensive care – a level of patient care that provides almost constant attention

internship – a period of training and practice to learn a profession on the job

monitor – to check on or keep track of for a particular reason

motor – related to motion or movement

orthopedic – related to medical practices and treatments involving bones and other parts of the body's skeletal structure

outpatients – patients who visit a doctor's office, clinic, or hospital for medical care but do not stay there overnight

outreach programs – organized efforts by knowledgeable professionals to provide information and services to the public, either free of charge or at a low cost

pediatric – related to medical practices and treatments involving the diseases, development, and overall care of children

polio – a dangerous, infectious disease that inflames nerve cells in the brain, causing muscle damage that can result in deformities, disabilities, or paralysis

prerequisite – a requirement that must be fulfilled before proceeding with other related activities

private practices – businesses in which professionals are self-employed, which means they work for themselves and personally take on all business-related risks and benefits

psychologists – people who are trained in the science of the mind and human behavior and are licensed to treat mental, emotional, and behavioral disorders

radiologists – medical doctors who are specially trained in the use of X rays and X-ray equipment

registered nurses – trained nurses who have graduated from an accredited nursing program and have been licensed by a government authority

residency – a stage of medical education during which a licensed doctor pursues advanced training in a medical specialty

shifts – scheduled periods of time when certain groups of workers are on duty

sibling – brother or sister

smallpox – a contagious, often fatal, viral disease that causes high body temperatures and eruptions, or blisters, on the skin

social workers – trained professionals who help people with severe economic and social problems

sprains – painful joint injuries caused by sudden or violent twisting, stretching, or tearing of muscles or ligaments

tantrum – an outburst of bad temper

therapy – the application of methods or procedures for treating physical, mental, emotional, or behavioral disorders

trauma – severe physical, mental, or emotional stress due to a painful event or injury

vaccinate – to inject a virus into a person's body to help the person resist a disease caused by the virus

vital signs – heart rate, blood pressure, body temperature, and other essential signs that a body is alive

wholesome – healthy and safe for body, mind, and spirit

World Health Organization – an agency of the United Nations that was established to prevent and eliminate disabling and deadly diseases around the world

Further Information

This book does not cover all of the jobs that involve working with children. Many jobs are not mentioned, including babysitter, nanny, and social worker. This book does, however, give you an idea of what working with children is like.

It is natural for most people to love children and enjoy playing with them, but that is not the same as working with children all day, every day. To work with children, you need to be a special type of person. You have to be able to put yourself in the child's position and have an idea of how the child feels. Most of all, you have to maintain your understanding and patience, even when children are being difficult and demanding.

The only way to decide if working with children is right for you is to find out what this kind of work involves. Read as much as you can about child-related careers and talk to people, especially people you know, who work with children.

When you are in middle school or high school, a teacher or career counselor might be able to help you arrange some work experience in a certain career. For careers working with children, that experience could mean babysitting, volunteering with youth groups or children's play groups, or helping out at a nursery school, a day care center, or the pediatric unit of a hospital, watching what goes on and how people who work there spend their time.

Books

Cool Careers without College for People Who Love to Work with Children
Harriet Webster
(Rosen, 2003)

Pediatrician
Rosemary Wallner
(Capstone Press, 2000)

Teacher
Peggy J. Parks
(Gale Group, 2003)

Web Sites

Hobsons CollegeView Career Center: Child Care Worker
www.collegeview.com/
career/careersearch/
job_profiles/human/
cc01.html

kidsnewsroom.com: Kids & Careers! (Amy: a physical therapist)
www.kidsnewsroom.com/
careers/careers.asp

Vocational Information Center: Early Childcare and Education Career Guide
www.khake.com/
page15.html

Useful Addresses

Child Care Worker

National Head Start Association
1651 Prince Street
Alexandria, VA 22314
Tel: (703) 739-0875
www.nhsa.org

Child Psychologist

American Psychological Association
750 First Street, NE
Washington, DC 20002-4242
Tel: (202) 336-5500 or (800) 374-2721
www.apa.org/students/

Child Therapist

The American Art Therapy Association
1202 Allanson Road
Mundelein, IL 60060-3808
Tel: (847) 949-6064 or (888) 290-0878
E-mail: info@arttherapy.org
www.arttherapy.org

American Music Therapy Association
8455 Colesville Road, Suite 1000
Silver Spring, MD 20910
Tel: (301) 589-3300
E-mail: info@musictherapy.org
www.musictherapy.org

American Speech-Language-Hearing
   Association (ASHA)
10801 Rockville Pike
Rockville, MD 20852
Tel: (800) 638-8255
www.asha.org

National Association for Drama Therapy
15 Post Side Lane
Pittsford, NY 14534
Tel: (585) 381-5618
www.nadt.org

Pediatrician

American Academy of Pediatrics
141 Northwest Point Boulevard
Elk Grove Village, IL 60007-1098
Tel: (847) 434-4000
www.aap.org

Pediatric Nurse

Pediatric Nursing Certification Board
800 S. Frederick Avenue, Suite 104
Gaithersburg, MD 20877-4150
Tel: (301) 330-2921 or (888) 641-2767
www.pncb.org

Preschool Teacher

National Association for the Education
   of Young Children
1509 16th Street, NW
Washington, DC 20036-1426
Tel: (202) 232-8777 or (800) 424-2460
www.naeyc.org

Schoolteacher

National Education Association
1201 16th Street, NW
Washington, DC 20036-3290
Tel: (202) 833-4000
www.nea.org

Index